MW01595088

Hello All! I would like to extend a warm welcome to each of you! I know that it is not a coincidence that you are here. but all part of Gods perfect plan. I am very blessed to have the privilege of serving our Heavenly Father through this women's ministry. I am a wife and "stay at home" mother of two yet, that does not define who I am, my identity in Christ does. As ladies, I know that we all live very busy lives, pressed with pressure to fill every hour of the day. I pray to be at peace with the choices I make on a daily basis because they align with Gods will for me and my family. I want nothing more than to use my gifts to further His kingdom, I want to choose joy, practice hospitality, walk humbly, look around with a generous eye, always speak seasoned with salt, trust His will and always be faithful. Easier said than done. I have to accept changes because everything changes, except His word. I read the bible not out of obligation, but to better know His word. If any of this sounds like the desire of your heart, join me on th's path and we will walk together.

~Kimberly Durham

Thank You's & Acknowledgements

Where do I even begin? First off, the words "thank you" doesn't begin to cut it, but here comes a small attempt from the heart.

The Lord, thank you for never giving up on me, for your gracious fury, and passionate love for this sinner. Thank you for leading me down a path that I don't deserve to be on, yet reminding me at every turn that "you alone will equip me."

Bo, for loving me like Jesus does. You are a patient, patient man and you will receive your full reward for this in Heaven.

Blanca and Katina, my original two Bible study lovelies, without y'all I would not be here. You have encouraged, strengthened, and kept me grounded. Katina, I miss you more than you know and I am a better person because of you.
Blanca, Bopsy...You are Ahhh-mazing!

"The Well" lovelies, to the core, you have been an answer to my prayers. Through thick and thin you have supported, and most of all, loved me. When I say I am praying for you, I am on my knees crying out for you. Confirmation 82 to put Esther on paper came from our sweet Yvonne and I am glad that her ear was fine-tuned to the Holy Spirit that day.

Andra Caldwell, I owe you so much that words seem inadequate. Thank you for pushing me and never allowing me to quit. You always remind me that someone has to step up and do what you know is right in your heart, even when you don't want to. Continue to live out Galatians 6:9, "So let's not get tired of doing what is good. At just the right time we will reap a harvest of blessing if we don't give up." It suits you and if it makes me smile, I know that Jesus is.

Taylor Caldwell...Seester...I am overwhelmed with LOVE for you. That is why I, literally, sob every time you move. The Lord is doing BIG things through you and Alan and I am enjoying watching you be the hands and feet of Jesus. Continue to walk in obedience.

Tom and Heather, thank you for answering the call on your lives to come to Columbus. If you had not listened to God's will for your life I would not be where I am today answering the call God had for me. Thank you for always being an encouragement.

Rhonda and Neil, the adopt-a-parents, I love y'all unconditionally. I know that I can come to you with anything and always be filled with Joy! Joy! Joy!

Shane Hall, my creative, talented, fabulous, Broadway dancing "brother." You are so dear and a huge inspiration to me. How would I live life without you? "When I stand before God at the end of my life, I would hope that I would not have a single bit of talent left, and could say, 'I used everything you gave me'. ~Erma Bombeck

Nicole Reigel, I am so blessed to call you friend. The Lord knew exactly what he was doing when he placed a designer-fashion-loving, interior-designing, Miss-America-watching, Lady of Leisure on my path, for you I am forever grateful.

We can make our plans, but The Lord determines our steps.

Proverbs 16:9

God opposes the proud and favors the humble.

James 4:6

Day 1

Before we start I would like to open us in prayer...
close one eye.

Dear Heavenly Father, thank you for this day. Thank you for leading us into this moment, this time you have created just for us to enjoy Your Word. Let us relish this moment. Open our Spiritual ears to hear, eyes to see, and heart to accept you wish to show us through Esther. It is all these things I pray in your precious Son's name,
Amen.

The story of Esther is set in the Persian Capital, Susa. Susa was a corrupt, worldly place and it was ruled by King Xerxes. Xerxes, known as "The Great" was the most powerful man on the Earth, wealthy beyond belief, and loved, loved, loved to flaunt his money. Let's open our bibles and **read Esther 1:1-9** and see what Xerxes did with all of that money.

So, what did he do?

How long did this last?

Whaaaat?! Who has that kind of vacation time saved up? This banquet was like an all-inclusive resort with the only rule being (vs. 8). This is probably why people did not complain about Xerxes being such a pompous prick.

They go into great detail about the castle & personally, I picture an even more glamorous version of my Restoration Hardware catalog. Rooms only decorated with the best white linens, porphyry (purple quartz), marble, mother-of-pearl, and other costly stones. It sounds absolutely stunning!

It amazes me the attention to detail that is shown in the few passages pertaining to the castle, yet we are going to see in the coming days that material possessions are the only thing that Xerxes is attentive to. **Take note of this.** Xerxes was a jerk in my book and we are about to see how much of a jerk he really is when he begins to throw his weight around or shall I say crown?!

Read Esther 1:10-22.

Beautiful Vashti, I am going to back track just a second. Vashti was originally Xerxes' sister-in-law... that's right... married to his BROTHER! Xerxes was so enthralled with her beauty that he took her as his own wife, but that's not all, he took his niece and married her as well! He had numerous wives but that didn't satisfy him so he also had a harem filled with thousands of women to fulfill his selfish desires.

Back to vs. 10 now. Eunuchs were special young men, why? They were chosen to watch over the women of the harem and castrated, yes castrated, so they would remain loyal to the king. Xerxes believed this would prevent the women of the harem from falling in love with and being abused by their caretakers. Xerxes told the 7 Eunuchs to bring Vashti to him so that she may "parade" her beauty around a bunch of drunken men. Some commentaries say Xerxes meant for her to be naked. Clothed or not, Xerxes showed slim to no respect for his wife.

Read 1 Corinthians 13:1-13.

As believers, we're to act differently and God encourages us to treat each other with respect and love. Xerxes made a rash decision by banishing Vashti and it is one he later regrets, as you'll see tomorrow. Poor decisions are often made on impulse as warned against in Proverbs 20:25. In opposition to this advice, Xerxes and his advisors were under the influence and allowed to make influential decisions that impacted the community. In Matthew 20:25-26, Jesus spoke with disapproval over the way some leaders "lord it over the people beneath them." King Xerxes and his advisors fell into this bad practice and issued edicts to force people to obey the law.

Day 2

Throughout Esther, God never appears, no scripture verses from other chapters are referenced, and no angels appear. So why is this book in the Bible?

Look up 2 Timothy 3:16 and record it below.

God tells us this and though we may not understand, God's plan is perfect.

Now read Esther 2:1-4.

Roughly 5 years have passed and what happened in vs. 1?

It took 5 years!! Really?!

What is the decision that his attendants came to agree upon?

That's right; bring in beautiful young virgins to compete for the crown just like a beauty pageant. The only difference is these girls get a full year at the day spa, for one night with the king.

Read Esther 2:5-7.

We have now met Mordecai and before we push forward, I want you to see a little history. Mordecai is Jewish and really Jews are not supposed to be in Susa; he is supposed to be in Jerusalem with the other Jews. If you are familiar with the book of Daniel, you know that God's people were punished and exiled by king Nebuchadnezzar. Why? It was God's punishment for their sins. Then came a good king, Cyrus, that ruled justly and he believed that no one should live in slavery, a decree was written and God's people were FREED! They were told by the prophet, Isaiah, to return to Jerusalem and rebuild the temple and city. Some did. Some did not. The temple was to be rebuilt and the presence of God would dwell there. To be away from Jerusalem was, in this time, to be out of the presence of God. Mordecai was one of the disobedient that stayed behind with

13

his family. You can read more about these accounts in Ezra and Nehemiah.

Read Esther 2:8-20.

Sweet, young, and beautiful Hadassah. Hadassah is her Jewish name, meaning star, but because they disobeyed by staying in Susa, she also had the Persian name of Esther. She is approximately 16-years old and she is now living in the harem, competing for one night with the king. This has to be a huge burden on a teenager.

On top of the anticipation of finding out if her chance with the king would be a success, Mordecai tells her to keep her nationality and background a secret. I am not sure about you, but I start singing "this little light of mine... hide it under a bushel?" No! No! No! Red Flag! We should never be told to keep our faith a quiet secret.

Record Ezekiel 3:11 in the space below and write how this verse speaks you.

I love that verse because it is a constant reminder to speak from the heart and the Lord will give you the boldness to approach others.

Esther was primped, primed, and pampered and I can almost guarantee that during that year she never followed any Jewish dietary restrictions. We also never see her leave for the temple or pray to God. After completing her prescribed beauty treatments (vs. 12), her number was finally called and guess what happens next (vs.18). Unfortunately, Esther continues to keep her nationality a secret as recommended by Mordecai.

Read Esther 2:21-23.

Mordecai has now overheard an assassination plot and has a big decision to make: keep his mouth closed and let the king die or tell and save the horrible man's life. He decides to tell and the two men were "done away with."

Where has all of this been recorded?

Take note of this book. We still hear nothing of what God is up to but there is no doubt God is there.

Let's pray.

Heavenly Father, You are Everlasting, the Prince of Peace and Providence. Continue to work in us as believers, Father. Help us to be bold in our faith so that we may shout your name! It's all these things I pray in Jesus' name,
Amen.

Day 3.

Delving right in to today, **let's read 3:1-2.**

Sometime Later, Xerxes promoted Haman. Keep in mind, Mordecai saved his life yet Haman is promoted to the most powerful official in the empire.

Verse 2 tells us as a sign of respect ALL of the king's officials were to, what?

Mordecai refused. Right now, you are probably thinking, why? Was it because he didn't get the promotion and was a little jealous or did he just not like Haman? Nope... History Lesson! In the Old Testament when God forms the nation of Israel the very first people to bust in and attack were the Agagites. Jews knew that "since the beginning" the Agagites wanted to kill them. Mordecai is a Jew and his new boss is Haman the Agagite, his arch enemy! This throws a wrench in the "keep our faith quiet" that Mordecai had been so stern on keeping up. It was the straw that broke the camel's back and it was not at the best time either. Up to this point he has not told anyone his nationality or let Esther claim the God of the Bible.

I know that I can relate to Mordecai here because there have been several times that I have kept my mouth shut and simply stewed inside only to erupt at the wrong time. Of course, this leaves everyone around to think, "What is wrong with this chick?!"

Do you have a tendency to speak at the wrong time or do you address this all differently? Share your experience below.

Read Esther 3:3-15.

I believe that Mordecai's faith was based on conviction. Sometimes doing what is right is not always smiled upon, but obeying God is more important, no matter what the timing.

Read Acts 5:29.

Mordecai the cowardly lion became courageous and stood up for what he believes in. I have a friend named, Bob that frequently says, "God works *on* unbelievers and *in* believers." This is Gods invisible hand at work IN Mordecai. He already believed he just needed to be bold.

What are your thoughts?

Mordecai attracted a lot of attention by refusing to bow and it wasn't enough for Haman to just fire him and move on. Haman learned of Mordecai's nationality and thought "BINGO! Here is my opportunity to do what my ancestors have tried and tried to do in the past, get rid of these pesky Jews." I really don't know what was going through his head, but this seems like it would be close. Haman went to the king and the decision to take action against ALL of the Jews was set. Signed and sealed with the king's signet ring. The signet ring was power of attorney, the same that had banished his ex-wife Vashti. They sent out swift messengers saying that all Jews young and old, including women and children, were to be slaughtered and annihilated on a single day, and the city of Susa fell into confusion. It sure seems a little harsh that all must die because one refused to bow. There is evil in this world, just waiting to get a hold of a signet ring, which I cannot even begin to imagine.

Let's pray.

Heavenly Father, today I am thankful, thankful for the blessings that you have given me. Thankful knowing that your invisible hand is always at work in our lives and that you work together for all good. Lord, continue to work in me just like you have worked in Mordecai. All these things I pray, in your Son's name, Amen.

Day 4

Turn on over to **Esther 4:1-11** and read up!

Public mourning. Public professing of faith. Public protesting. Well, isn't this a big change for Mordecai. In this chapter we are going to see Esther bloom where she has been planted. Both Esther and Mordecai are spiritually growing. We know that many times before a spiritual high, we are oftentimes humbled by our Mighty God. Here, Mordecai is terribly upset, wearing burlap and ashes to humble himself before our Lord.

How did Esther respond to this news (vs.4)?

Why do you think she felt that way?

She had absolutely no idea what was going on. She lives in the palace and, up to this point, no one knows she's Jewish to fill her in on the newly issue edict because it doesn't pertain to her. Esther sends Mordecai clothes, upon hearing of his wearing of sackcloth, and he refuses them. She wants to meet with him because she knows this is often a sign of mourning and sadness and she is probably a complete wreck. I know I would be. However, he cannot come into the palace in sackcloth because the king only wants (superficial) smiles and happiness in the castle.

Mordecai wants her to go to the king. However, she hasn't seen him, her HUSBAND, in how long (vs.11)?

Think she is happily married? Think again. Grass is not always greener folks.

Read Esther 4:12-17

I'm not sure about you, but does verse 13 sound a smidgen like a threat? I know I am taking some liberty here, but how would they know Esther was a Jew unless Mordecai was the one that told them? I am not sure how observant the attendants are, but I am sure they knew there was a family tie to the two. They just had to put the puzzle pieces together. You decide.

What do you think?

Mordecai commands his "daughter" to take action. What a turnaround. She is still keeping her faith private. She has been passive, Christian-loving Queen since she was "chosen" and now she is being called to be proactive!

Here blooms our Queen.

She rises up. She takes the reigns with "If I must perish, I must perish." She calls Mordecai to gather all the Jews and fast for 3 days. It is interesting to me that Esther chose 3 days. The same as our precious salvation to the redeeming resurrection. The kingdom of Heaven operates differently than the kingdoms of this world. And thankfully, the Lord walks beside us here.

Let's pray.

Dear Heavenly Father, protect us father, soften our hearts so that we ache for your people. Help us to love and strive to live to cry out, "If I must perish, I must perish" so your people can be unified to glorify Heaven. We love you, father. It's all these things I pray, in your precious Son's name,
Amen.

Day 5

Today we will watch Esther mature in her faith and become one of the true, great women of the Bible.

Read Esther 5:1-8.

Beautiful Esther had not been invited into the presence of her husband, the king, in over a month. She takes a bold step and walks into his throne room uninvited. I bet you could probably cut the awkward silence with a butter knife.

She came dressed in (vs.1) _____.

Royal robes were a sign of respect and Esther knew she had to take all the right steps in order to gain his favor. King Xerxes asks what she would like and even goes as far to say she may ask for up to half of the kingdom! This phrase is just the "polite" thing to say to his wife, whom he hasn't seen in 30 days, and in fact I would bet he'd be furious if she had taken him up on it.

Esther requests what from the king?

Who else was invited?

Now read Mark 6:14-29. What are some of the similarities you see in these stories?

These folks LOVE a good dinner party but it seems as if something bad always comes from them. Now back to our newly blossoming Esther!

Why do you think Esther didn't ask the king to save her people right then?

I think timing wasn't right. "We can make our plans, but the Lord determines our steps" Proverbs 16:9

Read Esther 5:9-14.

"God opposes the proud but gives favor and grace to the humble." This verse can be found many times in the bible: Proverbs 3:34, James 4:6, and 1 Peter 5:5. Hmm... you have to remember to never boast in yourself but Haman must have missed the memo. In the midst of his boasting he is reminded of the constant thorn in his side.

Read vs.13 again. What does he say to his wife?

A bit extreme, isn't it? And their solution to the problem is as equally extreme if not more! "Hey, let's set up a sharpened pole to impale him on and then you can go on your merry way." I am going to repeat that last line, "then you can go on your merry way." Whaaaat?! It is sad to me that his wife and friends have believed the false testimony Haman has told them and shaped their beliefs about Mordecai. They fall into the same hateful sin that Haman has become accustomed to. I am so thankful God is in control filled with gracious fury, love, and mercy. That he rules justly, aren't you? We should always let God handle our problems and enemies. Our lovely God recommends killing with kindness because that will "heap burning coals on his head" Romans 12:20. How awesome is that?!

Let's pray.

Father, thank you for working on the details of our lives so they may work out in your perfect timing. We are so broken and we need you as the glue that holds us together. Continue to refine us, so that all we see is your face. In your precious Son's name, Amen.

Day 6

'Furthermore, because we are united with Christ, we have received an inheritance from God, for he chose us in advance, and he makes everything work out according to His plan." Ephesians 1:11

Read Esther 6:1-9

How odd, how strange, and how ironic is it that the king couldn't sleep and read what had been done throughout his reign? I really want you to see this: reread and soak in verses 2-3. Coincidence? Nope. Providence. Providence is knowing that God is in control of all things. Haman had a little light bulb above his head in his "I know who that is" moment that allowed him to reach his peak in arrogance. "Who else could the king possibly be pleased with but me?" This is about to get good!

Read Esther 6:10-14.

Can you even imagine how upset he was when he found out it was the man he despised? Just the night before Haman was bragging about his position and the honor he had just received and now, he stands humiliated.

Turn to read James 4:13-16 and read the warning about bragging.

After the one man parade through the town, where does Mordecai go (vs. 12)?

Where does Haman go (vs. 12)?

You would have to admit that Haman at least has some of his priorities straight. He ran straight home to tell his wife about his humiliating morning and his wife and friends go on to say what's written in verse 13. That is kind of harsh too! Who are these people? One minute they want to impale Haman's enemy on a pole and the next they tell Haman at his lowest point that his enemy will surely bring him to ruin! It is important in our walk with Christ to not surround ourselves with people who will always tell us what we want to hear, how are we to grow? Accountability partners are crucial in spiritual grow because they keep us humble through a loving, Christ-centered relationship.

I want to end today with Proverbs 27:1, "Do not boast about tomorrow, for you do not know what a day may bring."

Dear Heavenly Father, help us to stay grounded in you. Keep us from a boastful and prideful spirit; keep our hearts humble and rooted in you. Thank you again for always loving us unconditionally. All these things I pray in Jesus' name,
Amen.

Day 7

"The Lord is not slow in keeping his promise, as some people think. No, He is patient for your sake. He does not want anyone to be destroyed, but wants everyone to repent." 2 Peter 3:9

Meditate on that verse and expect Him to speak to your heart. **Write down what he reveals below.**

Read Esther 7:1-5.

One little thing I have taken note of while traveling through this beloved book is every party they throw is a turning point. They are transitions. They make significant decisions while under the influence of alcohol that affects major people groups whether it is young, beautiful virgins or the Jewish. In verse 3 Esther FINALLY speaks out about her faith. But it was in God's timing so who can blame her? The king has no idea that she worships the God of the Bible and he doesn't really show a lot of emotion on the subject. Why? At the same time he is finding out that his right-hand man, most trusted advisor, and vice president of the palace has been less than loyal by trying to pull a fast one over on him.

Go ahead and read Esther 6:6-7.

The king storms out full of confusion, anger, and wrath... wrath can be ugggg-ly. Haman has been mad the majority of the time we have spent in Esther because a Jew would not bow to him, yet is it not ironic that now he is bowing at the feet of a Jew to plead for the sparing of his life?

Now read Esther 7:8-16. The anticipation is killing me!

In verse 8, my version says "assault" the queen, some say "molest" the queen. I doubt very seriously that Haman was putting the moves on Esther with everything going on in this moment. Maybe he tripped. Maybe he was so distraught he fell. Maybe he was begging like a toddler does by hanging on your poor little leg as you try to walk. I don't know, but the king was looking for a reason to kill him. Haman lied on God's people to kill them and now the great and powerful king is lying on him so that he can suffer the death he so proudly planned for Mordecai.

Harbona, the eunuch, casually walks by in verse 9 and says what?

Where is the pole? Oh yeah, Haman's front yard! Verse 10 blows me away like a leaf in the summer breeze. Haman was impaled...watch for it...the king's anger subsided...Bless it. It didn't even take 5 years this time!

God never misses a beat or wastes a word. "God works *on* unbelievers and *in* believers." Here we see this in action through unbelievers such as the king and the wonderful believer that Esther is.

Day 8

At any given moment you have the power to say this is not how the story is going to end in your own lives. As we come into chapter 8, Haman is dead. The death sentence for the Jews, however, looms over like a dark cloud. The Law of the Medes and Persians is still in effect and that law states that once a king makes a sovereign decree, sealed with the signet ring, it can never be reversed. Esther may have had her courageous moment, but she is still powerless.

Let's pray, before moving on.

Lord, I will always be amazed at how I am forgiven. Even though sometimes I cannot feel you beside me, all I have to do is open the bible and know you are here. Thank you for the outpouring of your favor and grace, love and mercy, and for making beautiful things out of dust and reminding me daily to lay down my life, pick up my cross and follow you. In Jesus' name,
Amen.

Read Esther 8:1-8.

I love that we are seeing Esther "grow up." From a 16-year old beautiful virgin to Queen of Susa, hero to the Jews, she is wise beyond her years now and God is clearly at work in her heart. I found such comfort knowing that at our weakest moment, when you have strayed so far, He will be there for you. Expect Him to.

Mordecai has now assumed Haman's position and is wearing the king's signet ring. You can visibly see favor and grace of God on his life. In verse 3, Esther comes to the king falling at his feet.

Why do you think she is so upset? Up until this point she hasn't been very emotional.

Read Esther 8:9-17.

Mordecai served the government faithfully for years. He put up with Haman's hatred and oppression and risked his life for his people. Mordecai is one of God's heroes. An exact reversal was written and sealed.

Record this decree below (vs. 11).

God's people rejoiced and celebrated!

**Verse 17 says, "And _____
became Jews. Many. Many. Many. Who all will one day be in the kingdom of God? That's right, many!**

Day 9

God can show up and change everything in an instant. This is not a promise that everything will change, but a promise that with God there is the possibility, always, that he could show up and reverse everything in an instant. Find hope in this.

Read Esther 9:1-19.

The body count was high. Day one: 500 men JUST in Susa died.

Go back and take note of verse 10.

This struck me as "I have seen this somewhere before." Here Esther is obeying and fulfilling a decree given to King Saul who disobeyed in 1 Samuel 15. Turn there.

What were the two things God tells Saul to do?
1. Kill the Agagites. They exist to destroy your people
2. Do not plunder

What does Saul do?
Lets them live and takes their goods as plunder.

I think it is safe to say that this whole story of Esther, by human perspective, should have never happened because Haman should have never been born. However, Esther reach MANY (remember them?) through her story.

Read Esther 9:20-32.

Jewish women were expected to be quiet, serve in the home, and stay on the fringe of political and spiritual life. Esther was a Jewish woman that broke through cultural norm, stepping outside her expected role. She was courageous and risked her life to help God's people, her people. God can use us, whatever our place in life. To celebrate Esther, Mordecai, and the Jews victory over Haman, they host a festival called Purim.

Day 10

Read Esther 10:1-3.

As we open to chapter 10, we are celebrating that this is not our home.

Look up and read Hebrews 13:14-15

In the end, God wins and His people rejoice. God rules the Heavens with love, grace, and mercy while King Xerxes rules with fear and intimidation, much like Satan. While God is working on King Xerxes through his helping of the Jews, his unbeliever tendencies still shine through by "impos[ing] a tax throughout the land even to the farthest shores." They may have been allowed to remain alive through Esther's influential position that God placed her in and her courage to stand up for her people, but the tax was double the previous amount. All recorded in The Book of the History of the Kings of Media and Persia (remember this from chapter 2?). This book is a historical account of truths that are not God breathed and often used for reference for additional information.

As we conclude the book of Esther, we have clearly seen God at work in the lives of individuals and in the affairs of a nation. We need to remember that even in our lives God works behind the scenes. We need to trust that He alone is in control, yet, we need to bloom where we are planted. Being content with where our lots have been cast in life can be hard, but God has us right where He wants us. Trust Him. We are His workmanship and he created us just for His good works. Spending time in His commands and glorifying Him through our lives is the least we can do in return. I can never repay Him, but I can live out John 3:35:

"Your heart for one another will prove to the world that you are my disciples."

And that is exactly what Esther did.

Before our final prayer together, I want to say thank you. Thank you for taking this journey into the unknown with me. I hope you enjoyed your time here and if you did, we would love to hear from you. Words of encouragement and prayers keep us on the path The Lord continues to light. Shine bright.

Let's pray.

Lord, open my eyes as I walk down this uncharted path. Cleanse my heart of any unrighteousness and disobedience; light my path brightly so that I may shine for you. I will be bold for you father, all to glorify your kingdom. Proverbs 16:9, "you can make your plans, but the Lord determines your steps." Hold me true to that promise. I have no plans, you alone are my fortress. Speak clearly and I will lend you my ear. Help me to recognize paths where righteous blooming may take place so your light may be shown bright for all to see. You alone are worthy. Thank you, Father.
Amen.

Perhaps, this is the moment for which you have been created.

Esther 4:14

All scripture
is God breathed
and profitable.

2 Timothy 3:16

Proof

Made in the USA
Charleston, SC
19 June 2014